T0025010

TRENDS IN SOUTHEAST ASIA

The **ISEAS – Yusof Ishak Institute** (formerly Institute of Southeast Asian Studies) is an autonomous organization established in 1968. It is a regional centre dedicated to the study of socio-political, security, and economic trends and developments in Southeast Asia and its wider geostrategic and economic environment. The Institute's research programmes are grouped under Regional Economic Studies (RES), Regional Strategic and Political Studies (RSPS), and Regional Social and Cultural Studies (RSCS). The Institute is also home to the ASEAN Studies Centre (ASC), the Singapore APEC Study Centre and the Temasek History Research Centre (THRC).

ISEAS Publishing, an established academic press, has issued more than 2,000 books and journals. It is the largest scholarly publisher of research about Southeast Asia from within the region. ISEAS Publishing works with many other academic and trade publishers and distributors to disseminate important research and analyses from and about Southeast Asia to the rest of the world.

THE NATIONAL RESEARCH AND INNOVATION AGENCY (BRIN)

A New Arrangement for Research in Indonesia

Ahmad Najib Burhani, Lilis Mulyani and Cahyo Pamungkas

ISSUE

18

2021

ISEAS YUSOF ISHAK INSTITUTE

Published by: ISEAS Publishing
                 30 Heng Mui Keng Terrace
                 Singapore 119614
                 publish@iseas.edu.sg
                 http://bookshop.iseas.edu.sg

© 2021 ISEAS – Yusof Ishak Institute, Singapore

All rights reserved. No part of this publication may be reproduced, stored in a retrieval system, or transmitted in any form, or by any means, electronic, mechanical, photocopying, recording or otherwise, without prior permission.

The authors are wholly responsible for the views expressed in this book which do not necessarily reflect those of the publisher.

ISEAS Library Cataloguing-in-Publication Data

Name(s): Burhani, Ahmad Najib, 1976–, author. | Mulyani, Lilis, 1976–, author. | Pamungkas, Cahyo, 1975–, author.
Title: The National Research and Innovation Agency (BRIN) : a new arrangement for research in Indonesia / by Ahmad Najib Burhani, Lilis Mulyani and Cahyo Pamungkas.
Description: Singapore : ISEAS-Yusof Ishak Institute, November 2021. | Series: Trends in Southeast Asia, ISSN 0219-3213 ; TRS18/21 | Includes bibliographical references.
Identifiers: ISBN 9789815011159 (soft cover) | ISBN 9789815011166 (pdf)
Subjects: LCSH: Research—Indonesia. | Government agencies—Indonesia.
Classification: LCC DS501 I59T no. 18(2021)

Typeset by Superskill Graphics Pte Ltd
Printed in Singapore by Mainland Press Pte Ltd

FOREWORD

The economic, political, strategic and cultural dynamism in Southeast Asia has gained added relevance in recent years with the spectacular rise of giant economies in East and South Asia. This has drawn greater attention to the region and to the enhanced role it now plays in international relations and global economics.

The sustained effort made by Southeast Asian nations since 1967 towards a peaceful and gradual integration of their economies has had indubitable success, and perhaps as a consequence of this, most of these countries are undergoing deep political and social changes domestically and are constructing innovative solutions to meet new international challenges. Big Power tensions continue to be played out in the neighbourhood despite the tradition of neutrality exercised by the Association of Southeast Asian Nations (ASEAN).

The **Trends in Southeast Asia** series acts as a platform for serious analyses by selected authors who are experts in their fields. It is aimed at encouraging policymakers and scholars to contemplate the diversity and dynamism of this exciting region.

THE EDITORS

Series Chairman:
   Choi Shing Kwok

Series Editor:
   Ooi Kee Beng

Editorial Committee:
   Daljit Singh
   Francis E. Hutchinson
   Norshahril Saat

The National Research and Innovation Agency (BRIN): A New Arrangement for Research in Indonesia

By Ahmad Najib Burhani, Lilis Mulyani and Cahyo Pamungkas

EXECUTIVE SUMMARY

- On 28 April 2021, the Indonesian government, under President Joko Widodo, dissolved the Ministry of Research, Technology, and Higher Education (Kemenristek-Dikti). Since then, the management of higher education has been taken over by the Ministry of Education and Culture, while research and innovation are now the responsibility of the National Research and Innovation Agency (Badan Riset dan Inovasi Nasional, or BRIN).
- Based on Presidential Regulation (Perpres) Nos. 33 and 78 of 2021, various research institutes, such as LIPI, BATAN, LAPAN and BPPT, and research agencies in some ministries have been or will be merged into BRIN, making it a "super-government agency" with an "overarching" role.
- With a Rp26 trillion budget allocated by the government for research per year and with a large number of researchers, BRIN is expected to boost national research and innovation, and help the country catch up with countries such as Singapore and South Korea.
- BRIN, however, faces some serious challenges. It is not related to budget, infrastructure or human resources, but to the research ecosystem and research culture of Indonesia. Technocratism, which has been restricting research in the country, will be its first challenge. Politicization of research institutions as indicated by the involvement of political parties in research supervision is another issue. Achieving an environment that makes good and healthy

research possible built around an effective system of funding, academic rewards, and a vibrant academic community, will be the third challenge.

- If BRIN manages to overcome these challenges sufficiently, it will be in a good position to enhance the capacity and competence of Indonesian researchers as the foundation for an advanced Indonesia by 2045.

The National Research and Innovation Agency (BRIN): A New Arrangement for Research in Indonesia

By Ahmad Najib Burhani, Lilis Mulyani and Cahyo Pamungkas[1]

INTRODUCTION

On 28 April 2021, President Joko Widodo (Jokowi) dissolved the Ministry of Research, Technology and Higher Education (Kemenristek-Dikti) and bestowed the authority to oversee research in the country upon the National Research and Innovation Agency (Badan Riset dan Inovasi Nasional, or BRIN). He also replaced Bambang Brodjonegoro as the head of BRIN, with Laksana T. Handoko, who was previously the head of the Indonesian Institute of Sciences (LIPI).

During his speech in front of Indonesian scientists in Busan, South Korea (25 November 2019), Jokowi stated that in the second term of his presidency, besides continuing the building of infrastructure, research and innovation would be his other focus and priority. He also revealed that he had established BRIN and that he hoped that it would become a "grand house" for national research.[2] Research institutions and various research

---

[1] Ahmad Najib Burhani is Visiting Senior Fellow at the ISEAS – Yusof Ishak Institute, Singapore and Research Professor at the National Research and Innovation Agency (BRIN), Jakarta. Lilis Mulyani and Cahyo Pamungkas are Senior Researchers at the Institute of Social Sciences and Humanities (ISSH), National Research and Innovation Agency (BRIN), Jakarta.

[2] CNBC Indonesia, "Mimpi Jokowi: Bangun Rumah Besar Penelitian", 25 November 2019, https://www.cnbcindonesia.com/news/20191125132519-4-117738/mimpi-jokowi-bangun-rumah-besar-penelitian (accessed 25 July 2021). Before being elected as president for the second term, Joko Widodo had

agencies in some ministries, including their budgets, will be consolidated into BRIN. Currently, Indonesia has in total a large budget for research and innovation, around Rp26 trillion[3] or US$69 million per year.[4] This is however "scattered" or distributed to several ministries and research agencies which sometimes conducted overlapping research.[5] Indonesia is also considered as having a low level of innovation. Based on the Global

---

included the establishment of a national research centre as one of his promises during the 2019 election campaign. "Berdasarkan Janji Kampanye, Apa Saja Lembaga yang Belum Dibentuk Jokowi?", https://nasional.kompas.com/read/2019/10/29/09512191/berdasarkan-janji-kampanye-apa-saja-lembaga-yang-belum-dibentuk-jokowi?page=all (accessed 18 August 2021).

[3] Regarding the total research budget of government research institutions and research units at state ministries, different numbers have been stated by the President of Indonesia, the Ministry of Finance, the Ministry of Research and Technology, and the head of BRIN. We note there are basically three different statements: total research budget of Rp26 trillion, Rp37 trillion, and Rp9.9 trillion (2021 budget according to the Ministry of Finance in November 2020). See Hanna Farah Vania, "Indonesia Belum Memandang Riset Sebagai Investasi", *katadata. co.id*, 25 November 2021, https://katadata.co.id/anshar/berita/5fbdc467818a1/indonesia-belum-memandang-riset-sebagai-investasi (accessed 26 July 2021); In his statement during an interview with *Kompas*, the head of BRIN mentions that the national budget for research is Rp37 trillion, which is bigger than the amount stated by the President. See "Laksana Tri Handoko: BRIN Dibentuk untuk Lebih Terbuka", *Kompas*, 17 May 2021, https://www.kompas.id/baca/ilmu-pengetahuan-teknologi/2021/05/17/laksana-tri-handoko-brin-dibentuk-untuk-lebih-terbuka (accessed 30 July 2021).

[4] Compared to Singapore, this budget is still low. Comparatively, Singapore budgets S$25 billion or 1 per cent of the nation's gross domestic product for five years (2021–25). https://www.straitstimes.com/singapore/record-25-billion-for-research-and-innovation-over-next-five-years-to-secure-singapores (accessed 19 August 2021).

[5] *Tempo*, "Jokowi Pertanyakan Hasil Riset dengan Anggaran Rp24.9 Triliun", 18 October 2019, https://bisnis.tempo.co/read/1077794/jokowi-pertanyakan-hasil-riset-dengan-anggaran-rp-249-triliun/full&view=ok (accessed 18 August 2021); CNN Indonesia, "Jokowi Minta Setop Program Riset yang Boroskan Anggaran", 11 December 2019, https://www.cnnindonesia.com/nasional/20191211193133-32-456164/jokowi-minta-setop-program-riset-yang-boroskan-anggaran (accessed 18 August 2021).

Innovation Index, Indonesia ranks 85th out of 131 countries. In Southeast Asia, East Asia and Oceania, Indonesia ranks 14th out of 17 countries.[6] This has been a cause for worry among its leaders; without effective research and innovation, Indonesia cannot compete in the global arena.

To overcome shortcomings in national research and innovation, Jokowi issued Presidential Decree No. 33 of 2021 (28 April 2021) and then revised it with Presidential Decree No. 78 of 2021 (24 August 2021) on BRIN. One point in the decree states that all research agencies, such as LIPI, the Agency for the Assessment and Application of Technology (BPPT), the National Nuclear Energy Agency (BATAN), and the National Institute of Aeronautics and Space (LAPAN), and research agencies in some ministries will be merged, or "integrated", to use the official term, into BRIN.

Following the dissolution of the Ministry of Research, Technology and Higher Education (Kemenristek-Dikti) and the appointment of L.T. Handoko as the head of BRIN, there were some simultaneous discussions on the future of research and innovation in the country under the umbrella of BRIN. Some scholars, such as Sofian Effendi, vice-chairman of the Indonesian Academy of Sciences (AIPI), saw that BRIN would not have the same level of authority as the state ministry in terms of accessing the government budget and communicating with the president.[7] This means that the government decision to dissolve the Kemenristek-Dikti and bestow the responsibility of managing, supervising, and regulating national research downgrades the status of national research and, at the same time, contradicts the president's statement in Busan.

Besides the level of authority, with the merger of various research agencies and the research institutes of some ministries, BRIN potentially becomes a "super government agency" in terms of human resources and

---

[6] Soumitra Dutta, Bruno Lanvin and Sacha Wunsch-Vincent, *Global Innovation Index 2020: Who Will Finance Innovation* (Ithaca: Cornell University, INSEAD, and the World Intellectual Property Organization, 2020).

[7] "BRIN Perlu Fokus Sinergikan Seluruh Ekosistem Riset", https://www.kompas.id/baca/ilmu-pengetahuan-teknologi/2021/06/18/brin-perlu-fokus-sinergikan-seluruh-ekosistem-riset (accessed 25 July 2021).

infrastructure.[8] The merging process could be a problem though; how long will it take this new agency to consolidate itself?

The next issue hotly debated in the academic community is the politicization of research or the relation between state or state ideology and the management of research. This is particularly related to the point in the presidential decree stipulating that the head of the supervisory board of BRIN "in *ex-officio* comes from someone in the Supervisory Board of the institution that carries out government duties in the education of the Pancasila ideology" (*secara ex-officio berasal dari unsur Dewan Pengarah badan yang menyelenggarakan tugas pemerintah di bidang pembinaan ideologi Pancasila*). Currently, the head of the Supervisory Board of the Agency for Pancasila Ideology Education (BPIP) is Megawati Soekarnoputri, the chairperson of the Indonesian Democratic Party – Struggle (PDI-P).

With various controversies around BRIN, this writing, therefore, intends to, first, briefly map and describe the historical trajectory and development of research agencies in Indonesia since Independence in 1945. The dynamics of the establishment of BRIN is the second elaboration of the writing. Third and last, it discusses the prospects and challenges of research and innovation in Indonesia under BRIN. The questions that will be dealt with in this writing are the following: What are the main obstacles BRIN faces in achieving its goals? What has made research and innovation in Indonesia appear stagnant or "achieving nothing", as stated in Joko Widodo's statement? What was and is the relation between research and politics in Indonesia?

THE ORGANIZATION OF RESEARCH

Andrew Goss in *The Floracrats* (2011) wrote that the institutionalization of scientific research in Indonesia had begun in the colonial period.[9]

---

[8] " 'Superagency' May Further Politicize Indonesian Research", https://www.sciencemag.org/news/2021/04/superagency-may-further-politicize-indonesian-research (accessed 25 July 2021).

[9] Andrew Goss, *The Floracrats: State-Sponsored Science and the Failure of the Enlightenment in Indonesia* (Madison: University of Wisconsin Press, 2011).

In 1790, some Dutch Indies scholars founded an association to spread the idea of enlightenment to the public; this was the Batavian Society for Art and Science. This organization did not develop until the mid-1830s, with the reprinting of papers and articles from journals in Europe. However, as stated by Goss, this organization failed in institutionalizing knowledge, popularizing the idea of enlightenment or developing civil society in the colonial hierarchy. Many naturalists then began to develop botanical research at the Bogor Botanical Gardens as a natural history project. Although the colonial government ignored their activities and their reach was limited to a few educated Europeans, they successfully conducted research on export crops. At the end of the nineteenth century, the colonial government began to invite naturalists to work as colonial officials and these became the first intellectuals to work with the government. The naturalists were generally members of the Botanical Garden (S' Lands Plantentuin te Buitenzorg) established in 1817. The colonial government then established the Netherlands Indies Natural Sciences Center in 1928. After the end of the Second World War, in 1948, this centre was transformed into the Organization for the Study of Natural Sciences, which persisted until 1956.[10]

After the Dutch recognized Indonesian sovereignty in 1949, Dutch scientists left Indonesia, creating a vacuum in the institutionalization of research and the development of knowledge. According to Asvi Warman Adam, in 1952, President Sukarno assigned Sarwono Prawirohardjo, a medical doctor and formerly chairman of Jong Java in 1927, to found a research institute. In 1956, the Indonesian Science Council (Majelis Ilmu Pengetahuan Indonesia, or MIPI) was established through Law No. 6 of 1956.[11] In 1962, it came under the Ministry of National Research Affairs (Departemen Urusan Riset Nasional, or Durenas), and the Head of MIPI

[10] Mayling Oey-Gardiner, "Study of the Role of the Indonesian Institute of Sciences (LIPI) in Bridging Between Research and Development Policy", PT Insan Hitawasana Sejahtera, Jakarta, August 2010.

[11] Asvi Warman Adam, *Sarwono Prawirohardjo: Pembangun Institusi Ilmu Pengetahuan di Indonesia* (Jakarta: LIPI Press, 2009).

was now the deputy minister of research. The government assigned MIPI to establish and maintain several national research institutions; Durenas then became the National Research Institute (Lembaga Riset Nasional, or Lemrenas) until 1966.

During this period, the government established two research institutions: the National Atomic Energy Agency (Badan Tenaga Atom Nasional, or BATAN) and the National Aeronautics and Space Agency (Lembaga Penerbangan dan Antariksa Nasional, or LAPAN). In 1954, the government formed the State Committee for Radioactive Investigations, which in 1958 became the Atomic Energy Institute. It was not until 1964, through Law No. 31 of 1964, that this institution became BATAN.[12] In addition, the government through the First Minister, Juanda, also formed the Astronautics Committee, which in 1963 became LAPAN through Presidential Decree No. 236 of 1963.[13]

After the transfer of power from President Sukarno to Suharto in 1967, the government dissolved Lemrenas and MIPI through Presidential Decree No. 128 of 1967. Then, based on MPRS Decree No. 18 of 1967, the government established the Indonesian Institute of Sciences (Lembaga Ilmu Pengetahuan Indonesia, or LIPI) to accommodate the tasks of Lemrenas and MIPI. LIPI has the following tasks: (1) to guide the development of science and technology rooted in Indonesia for the welfare of the Indonesian people; (2) to seek scientific truth where scientific freedom, freedom of research, and freedom of the pulpit are recognized and guaranteed, as long as they do not conflict with Pancasila and the 1945 Constitution, and; (3) to prepare the establishment of the Indonesian Academy of Sciences.[14]

---

[12] "Sejarah BATAN", http://www.batan.go.id/index.php/id/home/sejarah (accessed 25 July 2021).

[13] "Sejarah LAPAN", https://www.lapan.go.id/page/sejarah-lapan (accessed 25 July 2021).

[14] Oey-Gardiner, "Study of the Role of the Indonesian Institute of Sciences (LIPI)".

In addition to LIPI, the government also established the Agency for the Assessment and Application of Technology (BPPT) through Presidential Decree No. 25 of 1978. This agency was developed from Pertamina's (National Corporation of Oil and Gas) Advanced Technology Division which was formed in 1976 and Pertamina's Advanced Aviation Technology and Technology Division (ATTP) which came into being in 1974.[15] By 1978, therefore, Indonesia had four national research institutions, namely LIPI, BATAN, LAPAN and BPPT, each with specific tasks—LIPI aimed to foster the development of science, while BATAN, LAPAN and BPPT focused on development, research and utilization of atomic energy, aerospace and aviation technology.

The mandate to establish the Indonesian Academy of Sciences (Akademi Ilmu Pengetahuan Indonesia, or AIPI) began in 1969 with LIPI's Memorandum for establishing AIPI, but the national government did not follow it up. It was not until 1983 that the Minister of Research and Technology revived the idea of establishing AIPI by forming a committee to prepare an academic draft. Finally, in 1990 AIPI was established through Law No. 8 of 1990. This is an independent and non-structural forum for leading scientists, and not a government agency or part of a government agency. It formulates directions and solves problems related to the mastery, development and utilization of science and technology.[16]

After the *Reformasi* or Reform Movement in 1998, the Government through Law No. 18 of 2002 established the National Research Council (Dewan Riset Nasional, or DRN), whose task was to support the Minister of Research and Technology in formulating direction, priorities and policies in the field of science and technology development. The tasks of AIPI and DRN had many similarities and overlaps. In order to streamline the bureaucracy, the government dissolved DRN in 2020.

---

[15] "Sejarah", https://www.bppt.go.id/profil/sejarah (accessed 25 July 2021).

[16] Asvi Warman Adam, *Sarwono Prawirohardjo*, pp. 59–67; Tri Nuke Pudjiastuti, *50 Tahun Kiprah LIPI untuk Bangsa* (Jakarta: LIPI Press, 2017), p. 15; "Merunut Jejak Sejarah Pembentukan AIPI", https://aipi.or.id/ (accessed 14 August 2021).

Tracing in further detail, the end of the New Order also marked the end of Sciences and Technology (ST) mainstreaming in the development agenda and in public discourse. During the New Order, President Suharto supported the Minister of Research and Technology and the head of BPPT, BJ Habibie, in developing ST by establishing the Agency for Strategic Industries (Badan Pengelola Industri Strategis, or BPIS).[17] However, his regime ended in 1998 and the government under Megawati dissolved BPIS in 2003 and President Abdurrahman Wahid changed the course of ST from "high tech" to "technology for the people" by appointing Muhammad A.S. Hikam as Minister of Research and Technology (1999–2001).[18] After that, no president continued the mainstreaming of ST due to that policy's linkage to the New Order and BJ Habibie, the right-hand man of Suharto in the development of Science, Technology, and Innovation. As we have seen, when the Joko Widodo administration revived the policy on Science and Technology, it did so by linking it to the first President, Soekarno, and not to Habibie.

The institutionalization and management of science and technology entered a new phase with Law No. 11 of 2019 concerning the National System of Science and Technology. This law mandates the government to establish the National Research and Innovation Agency (BRIN). The government then issued Presidential Decree No. 74 of 2019 regarding the establishment of BRIN, which then experienced a tug of war between political interests until the birth of a new Presidential Regulation, namely Presidential Decree No. 33 of 2021 and No. 78 of 2021. According to the

---

[17] Sulfikar Amir, *The Technological State in Indonesia: The Co-constitution of High Technology and Authoritarian Politics* (London & New York: Routledge, 2013).

[18] F. Harry Sampurno-Kuffal, *Keruntuhan Industri Strategis Indonesia* (Jakarta: Khasanah Bahari, 2011); Topan Yuniarto, "Kebijakan Riset dan Teknologi: Dari Soekarno hingga Jokowi", *Kompas*, 9 August 2021, https://kompaspedia. kompas.id/baca/paparan-topik/kebijakan-riset-dan-teknologi-dari-soekarno-hingga-jokowi (accessed 19 August 2021).

provisions of these two Presidential Regulations, four Non-Ministerial Government Institutions (LPNK), namely LIPI, BATAN, LAPAN and BPPT, will be the implementing organizations for research, development and assessment under the umbrella of BRIN.[19]

The formation of BRIN was followed by the dissolution of the Ministry of Research and Technology and Higher Education (Kemenristek-Dikti). This dissolution marks the end of a long-standing dualism in government policies related to research. Historically, as mentioned above, the government formed the Ministry of National Research Affairs in 1962, which became the State Ministry of Research in 1973 and which finally changed its name to the State Ministry of Research and Technology in 1986. After the *Reformasi*, in 2004, the nomenclature of the ministry became the Ministry of Research and Technology. At the beginning of President Joko Widodo's administration in 2014, the Directorate General of Higher Education was merged with this ministry to create the Ministry of Research, Technology, and Higher Education. However, in 2021, President Joko Widodo returned the directorate general of Higher Education to the Ministry of Education and Culture.[20] Consequently, the function of research and innovation policy is now the responsibility of BRIN, but research policy on campus is under the authority of the

---

[19] Law No. 11 of 2019 on Sisnas Iptek, the basis for the establishment of BRIN has been brought before the Constitutional Court. The interpretation of the word *terintegrasi* (integrated) in the Article 48 (paragraph 1) of the Law, i.e., "To carry out an Integrated Research, Development, Assessment and Application, as well as Invention and Innovation, a national research and innovation agency is formed", as understood by the government, was contested by Heru Susetyo, a member of the Regional Research Council, Jakarta Branch. The first hearing of the judicial review was on 21 September 2021. See "Sidang Perkara Nomor 46/PUU-XIX/2021. Selasa, 21 September 2021", https://www.youtube.com/watch?v=QGrrnlDjAC8 (accessed 22 September 2021).

[20] Yanuar Nugroho, "Riset dan Inovasi di Simpang Jalan", *Kompas*, 15 April 2021, https://www.kompas.id/baca/opini/2021/04/15/riset-dan-inovasi-di-simpang-jalan (accessed 25 July 2021).

directorate general of higher education at the Ministry of Education, Culture, Research and Technology.[21]

In addition to government research institutions and those that are part of the government, universities, both public and private, spread throughout Indonesia, also carried out research, development studies, and the application of science and technology. Research fields in universities covered ten topics regulated in the National Research Master Plan: food, energy, health, transportation, information and communication technology, defence and security, advanced materials, maritime, disaster, and social sciences-humanities.[22] Research in universities has also determined the Tingkat Kesiapan Teknologi (TKT) or Technological Readiness Level from TKT 1 (basic research) to 9 (full commercial application or technology on general availability for all consumers). Between 2014 and 2021, the management of universities was under the Directorate General of Higher Education, which was at that time still under Kemenristek-Dikti, a situation that facilitated the coordination of national research activities.

Apart from universities, research is also proliferating in the corporate and non-government sectors, which tend towards practical innovations for solving problems faced by the business world and society. In social research, the Center for Strategic and International Studies (CSIS) has existed since 1970, and the SMERU Research Institute has focused on research in socio-economics since 2001. Likewise, the Institute for Economic and Social Research, Education and Information (LP3ES), established in 1971, has a long history of managing academic publications, such as *Prisma* magazine. In contrast to LPNK or research

---

[21] According to Presidential Regulation No. 31 of 2021 on the Management of the Role and Function of the Ministry of Education, Culture, Research, and Technology and the Ministry of Investment; and Presidential Regulation No. 32 of 2021 on the Amendment of Presidential Regulation No. 68 of 2019 on State Ministries Organizations.

[22] Ministry of Research, Technology, and Higher Education, *National Research Master Plan 2017–2045* (Jakarta: Ministry of Research, Technology, and Higher Education 2017), http://rirn.ristekdikti.go.id (accessed 25 July 2021).

institutions under universities, these research institutions have developed by seeking funding sources, either through collaboration with the government or international donor agencies. Because of their flexibility, they often respond more quickly to social phenomena and advance policy recommendations that become a reference for policymakers. Research centres in government institutions have to go through long bureaucratic procedures of submitting budgets, research collaborations and publications. Meanwhile, social phenomena change rapidly, and therefore requires studies that can be done quickly.[23]

NATIONAL RESEARCH AND INNOVATION AGENCY (BRIN)

a. The Onset of BRIN

In this section, we will discuss the onset of the establishment of BRIN. This includes a timeline analysis of the first initiative of Law No. 18 of 2002 revision, started in late 2015. We will also show how this initiative went through the political process at the People's Representative Body (DPR RI), and received support from Indonesia's largest political party, PDI-P, under its prominent leader, Megawati Sukarnoputri.

---

[23] As mentioned in Oey-Gardiner, "Study of the Role of the Indonesian Institute of Sciences (LIPI)", many researchers under the social and humanity division of the Indonesian Institute of Sciences are generally mediocre in terms of publications. It means that their publications are neither very high or low in scientific quality, and most policymakers do not refer to them. Furthermore, according to the *2020 Global Go To Think Tank Index* (GGTTI) published by Lauder Institute at the University of Pennsylvania, the nine best policy research in Indonesia are Center for International and Strategic Studies (CSIS), Economic Research Institute for ASEAN (ERIA), Center for International Forestry Research (CIFOR), Indonesian Corruption Watch (ICW), Institute of National Capacity Studies (INCS), Center for Indonesian Policy Studies (CIPS), SMERU Research Institute, PATTIRO and Partnership Governance Reform. No government or campus-based research institute in Indonesia are included. See James G. McGann, "2020 Global Go To Think Tank Index Report", 28 January 2021, p. 18, https://repository.upenn.edu/think_tanks/18https://repository.upenn.edu/cgi/viewcontent.cgi?article=1019&context=think_tanks

Figure 1: Logo of BRIN, Launched on National Technology Awakening Day, 10 August 2021

The very first recorded sign of initiative was when the National Forum of Research Professors (Forum Nasional Profesor Riset, or FNPR)[24] met with Megawati on 15 March 2018.[25] FNPR's main agenda was to re-emphasize the urgent need for reform in research and technology management in Indonesia and to encourage this in the National System of Science and Technology Bill (RUU Sinas Iptek), which was then being discussed. The research and innovation community in Indonesia showed concern over the lack of government and legislative support to enhance research and innovation.

---

[24] The National Forum of Research Professor was created on 9 November 2017. It gathers research professors from different research institutions and state ministries and has as its main objective the development of a conducive environment for scientific research and development, http://lipi.go.id/berita/single/Forum-Profesor-Riset-Nasional-Terbentuk-Ini-Harapannya-ke-Depan/19405 (accessed 9 July 2021).

[25] "Belasan Pakar Apresiasi Keberpihakan Megawati pada Riset", *Liputan6.com*, 15 March 2018, https://www.liputan6.com/news/read/3376098/belasan-pakar-apresiasi- keberpihakan-megawati-pada-riset (accessed 30 July 2021).

The research and innovation community saw an opportunity in a proposal to revise Law No. 18 of 2002. The Bill on the Sinas Iptek Law revision was seen as one answer to the unsettled deficiency of Indonesia's research and innovation, as explained in the previous section. To help pass the Bill, political commitment and support from Indonesia's largest political party at that time was urgently needed. The PDI-P under Megawati held the majority of seats in the DPR RI, and was considered the ideal supporter for the draft Bill to be endorsed by the government of Indonesia (Kemenristek-Dikti together with LIPI and BBPT). The draft bill also received wide support from Himpenindo, the National Association of Indonesian Researchers.

During the meeting, the leader of the National Forum of Research Professors, Syamsudin Haris, a prominent political scientist, emphasized that research and technology authority must be directly under the President's supervision. This meeting also mentioned the need for a National Research Agency (Badan Riset Nasional).[26] Megawati agreed with the NFRP that a single authoritative state agency managing research and technology could help achieve the aims of Golden Generation 2045 (100 years of Indonesian Independence),[27] and put Indonesia among high-income countries in 2045.

Prior to 2016, there were several draft bills prepared to replace Law No. 18 of 2002 on National System of Research, Development and Application of Science and Technology, among others: draft Bill on Researcher and Scientific Research (RUU Peneliti dan Penelitian Ilmu Pengetahuan, or RUU PPIP) prepared by LIPI, and draft Bill on National System of Science and Technology prepared by the Kemenristek-Dikti. LIPI and BPPT were later invited to be part of the Inter-Ministries Committee (Panitia Antar Kementerian) of the Bill on Sinas Iptek.

---

[26] During this period, the term was still unconfirmed and was continuously changing. The term BRIN had not been coined yet.

[27] "Usul Bentuk Badan Riset Nasional, Megawati Ingin Negara Berdikari", *Sindonews.com*, 15 March 2018, https://nasional.sindonews.com/berita/1289940/12/usul-bentuk-badan-riset-nasional-megawati-ingin-negara-berdikari/ (accessed 30 July 2021).

The Ministry, LIPI and BPPT finally agreed to work together on one comprehensive draft in early 2016. The competitive tension between LIPI and BPPT was quite apparent at the discussion, with both claiming to be the authoritative body for research (LIPI) and for the application of science (BPPT). Meanwhile, the Ministry's role appeared mainly to be about maintaining coordination between agencies and providing the national research agenda/policy. This was also one of the reasons there was ambiguity in the management of science and technology in the approved Law No. 11 of 2019, particularly regarding which the leading authority of science and technology management was.

The inter-agency committee responsible for preparing the draft to revise Law No. 18 of 2002 highlighted the weaknesses of that law. First, it presented no inter-agency and inter-sector coordinating mechanism, particularly at the level of national agenda setting and policy planning on science and technology. Second, the law did not clearly regulate human resource capacity-building, institutional arrangements including research and development budgeting systems, and science and technology audits. Third was the urgent need to regulate material transfer agreements between national research agencies with its research partners.[28] These weaknesses highlighted the need to revise the 2002 Law.

The revision of the 2002 Law also encouraged active promotion of the process and of a shift in focus to include as many relevant stakeholders as possible. The 2018 meeting between the National Forum of Research Professors and political stakeholders must be seen in this context and as the critical phase in the draft bill discussion. There were times when the Bill was on the bottom of the list in the National Legislation Programme (Program Legislasi Nasional, or Prolegnas); this condition showcased the need for political support to finish the draft. The period between 2016 to 2018 was a critical moment for the scientific community in Indonesia;

---

[28] Meeting notes, Inter-Agencies Committee (Panitia Antar Kementerian), "Rapat Pembahasan Rancangan UU Peneliti dan Ilmu Pengetahuan dan RUU Revisi UU Sistem Nasional Penelitian, Pengembangan dan Penerapan Ilmu Pengetahuan dan Teknologi", Jakarta, 3 February 2016.

the draft bill was under intensive discussion and was said to signify a major transformation in the management of research and technology in Indonesia.

b. The Sinas Iptek Law: A Compromised Outcome

The attitude of the scientific community to keep its distance from politics and law-making in previous decades resulted in the lack of government and political support for the development of science, technology and innovation. Among the inherited impacts are, *first*, the low government budget on science and technology development; *second*, the lack of understanding for government research institutions and research processes among policymakers; and *third*, the disintegration of research and innovation institutions. It was because of these reasons that the research community, particularly the Kemenristek-Dikti, with LIPI, BPPT and the Association of National Researcher (Himpenindo), put in more effort to accelerate the law-making process at DPR RI.

Law No. 11 of 2019 was passed by the House of Representative's General Meeting on 16 July 2019 and signed into law on 13 August 2019 by Joko Widodo. Several provisions of the law suggest that the outcome of the law was a compromise between different interests during the process. Among the important outcomes was the division of research, development, assessment and application (*penelitian, pengembangan, pengkajian dan penerapan*, also known as *litbangjirap*), reflecting the compromised outcome between LIPI and BPPT.

The new law defines science and technology institutional management as an entity that creates a relationship among organizations or a group of people to collaborate.[29] During the process from draft bill to approved law, numerous explanations were given about the division between research

---

[29] In the draft bill, national research and technology management was drafted under Chapter V (draft Bill dated 19 February 2016). Meanwhile, following the approval, the institutional arrangement for an authoritative body to manage science and technology is regulated under Chapter VI (Articles 42–48).

and development (*litbang*) and assessment and application (*jirap*). The end result depicts the competition and, finally, the compromised result between LIPI and BPPT. As explained earlier, many institutions (including LIPI and BPPT) sought to maintain a position in the national research institutional arrangement that was secured from the revised law; they had previously only been regulated under Presidential Decree.

The objective to create an integrated research institution also affects the dissolution of existing bodies such as the Ministry of Research and Technology and the National Research Council (DRN). Ambiguity regarding the institutional arrangement for science and technology remains as details are sparse within the new law. This includes details on the establishment of a national research and innovation agency (BRIN). The new BRIN aims to integrate—or "consolidate", the term commonly used by the head of BRIN—the *litbangjirap* functions under one body. The function, responsibility, and authority of the Kemenristek-Dikti was given to the Central Government in Law No. 11 of 2019. These functions are those related to the formulation of a national agenda for science and technology (Rencana Induk Pemajuan Iptek)[30] and other functions such as to increase human-resource capacity in research and technology.[31]

Who actually represents the "central government" as mentioned in the Law is unclear. In Article 1, the central government is defined the President of the Republic of Indonesia as the highest authoritative executive power, followed the Vice President and the Minister as mentioned in the Indonesian 1945 Constitution. In this law, there is no clear indication which Minister is assigned to help the President and Vice President in dealing with research and technology matters. This is solid

---

[30] Previously under the DRN it was called Rencana Induk Riset Nasional (RIRN).

[31] The early draft Bill of Law No. 18 of 2002 revision (January 2016 draft version) still mentioned the Ministry of Research, Technology, and Higher Education in each of the central government coordinating function. However, the final draft (including those being approved into Law No. 11 of 2019) replaced "Ministry" with "Central Government". This marked the intention to abolish the Ministry for Research and Technology.

proof of the lawmakers' intention to dissolve Kemenristek-Dikti and establish a new national research agency.[32]

Further, the Law does not mention DRN as an important part of the national system of science and technology. DRN had been the board responsible for formulating the National Main Research Agenda (Rencana Induk Riset Nasional, or RIRN) according to Law No. 11 of 2002 and Presidential Regulation (Peraturan Presiden, or Perpres) No. 16 of 2005. However, in 2020, Perpres No. 112 of 2020 formally abolishes DRN. A discussion arose in 2020 on whether the function of DRN should be given to another body. The Indonesian Academy of Sciences (Akademi Ilmu Pengetahuan Indonesia, or AIPI), for example, was encouraged to take over the function of giving inputs and consideration on matters related to science and technology to the President.[33] The National Forum of Research Professors also suggested establishing a Science, Technology and Innovation Policy Board or Dewan Kebijakan Iptekin (DK Iptekin).[34]

c. BRIN Missions: Initial Observations of Its Implications

The establishment of BRIN in 2021 has three main implications: first, the merger of national (government) research institutions that manage science and technology; second, the integration of government research

---

[32] "Pemerintah Didorong Bentuk Lembaga Tinggi Pengelola Sumber Daya Iptek", *Kompas*, 23 February 2018, https://www.kompas.id/baca/utama/2018/02/23/pemerintah-didorong-membentuk-lembaga-tinggi-pengelola-sumber-daya-iptek (accessed 30 July 2021).

[33] Luthfi T. Dzulfikar, "Panel Ahli: Dewan Riset Nasional Dibubarkan, Apa Artinya Bagi Penelitian di Indonesia?", *The Conversation*, 20 December 2020, https://theconversation.com/panel-ahli-dewan-riset-nasional-dibubarkan-apa-artinya-bagi-penelitian-di-indonesia-152325 (accessed 30 July 2021).

[34] "Pemerintah Didorong Bentuk Lembaga Tinggi Pengelola Sumber Daya Iptek", *Kompas*, 23 February 2018, https://www.kompas.id/baca/utama/2018/02/23/pemerintah-didorong-membentuk-lembaga-tinggi-pengelola-sumber-daya-iptek/ (accessed 30 July 2021).

funding; and third, the re-emergence of an era of research and innovation objectives being directed for national ideology and economy.

There was not much written on BRIN before 2020 although it was explicitly mandated in Article 48 of Law No. 18 of 2019. Following the Law, the President released Presidential Decree (Keputusan Presiden) No. 113/P of 2019 regarding the establishment of state ministries in the Cabinet for the period 2019–24, wherein BRIN was included. That Decree was followed by Perpres No. 74 on BRIN. As stated in Article 36, this regulation was only valid until 31 December 2019. Another Presidential Regulation was then issued, i.e. Perpres No. 95 of 2019, to give a legal basis for the existence of the BRIN until 30 March 2020. There was a period of time (between 31 March 2020 to 28 April 2021) when there was a legal vacuum on the institutional arrangement for BRIN. It was not until the enactment of President Regulation No. 33 of 2021 on the National Research and Innovation Agency (BRIN) that discussions regarding the institutional arrangement of Indonesian science and technology management re-emerged.[35] This regulation was issued on 28 April 2021. Four months after the enactment of Presidential Regulation No. 33 of 2021, on 24 August 2021, this regulation was revised through the issuance of Presidential Regulation No. 78 of 2021, stating in page 1 (Consideration) that the previous regulation still had "shortcomings and has not accommodated the development and needs of national research and innovation … so it needs to be replaced".

---

[35] The Presidential Regulation was signed by President Joko Widodo on 28 April 2021. It is important to note that research and innovation were strongly and heavily mentioned in the bill on the Pancasila Ideology Guidelines (HIP). Although the bill does not mention BRIN, it mentions in Article 35 paragraph 2, that "In order to ensure the implementation of the Pancasila Ideology Guidelines in the national system of science and technology as referred to in paragraph (1), a national research and innovation ministry/agency is formed to carry out research, development, study, and application, as well as integrated inventions and innovations." However, because of the huge controversy and rejection during the deliberation, this bill was cancelled.

We find at least six main missions occasionally promoted by the newly appointed Head of BRIN, Laksana Tri Handoko. These are: to integrate research institution management; to create profit and strategic innovation; to develop a "research powerhouse"; to increase the capacity of scientific human resources; to improve the management of life sciences and intellectual property deriving from scientific research; to create and ensure a research and innovation ecosystem in the form of collaboration between government, researcher and DUDI (*dunia usaha dunia industri* or the business and industry sectors), and last but not least; to pool research and development budgets from different state ministries and increase its spending. See Figure 2.

Integrating research institution management under BRIN means that leading research institutions and all state research agencies in Indonesia will be merged. Aside from these institutions, BRIN will also consolidate all research, development, assessment and application of science and technology under its umbrella. This means that the state ministries or other central government bodies will transfer functions related to research (*penelitian*) to BRIN, including researchers and research budgets. This is a challenging task for BRIN. In terms of funding, currently, the total research budget is spread among different research agencies and state ministries. The allocated research budget for a state ministry can reach as much as Rp800 billion per year. With a total of thirty-four ministries, a total national budget for research and innovation can add up to Rp26 trillion annually. Such a research budget under one management is significant, reaching towards the target of 4.2 per cent of the annual GDP.[36]

Such an integration will be quite a challenge though. Spending on national research has often been criticized for mismanagement, and the Corruption Eradication Commission (KPK) found in 2018 that only 43.74 per cent of the research and development budget was

---

[36] CNBC Indonesia, "Mimpi Jokowi: Bangun Rumah Besar Penelitian".

Figure 2: Three Directions and Seven Targets of the Establishment of the BRIN

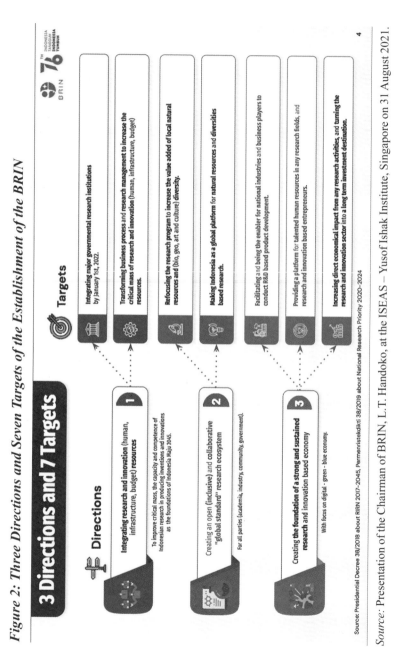

Source: Presentation of the Chairman of BRIN, L.T. Handoko, at the ISEAS – Yusof Ishak Institute, Singapore on 31 August 2021.

actually spent on research activities.[37] Based on this finding, the KPK suggests that BRIN strengthens its function as coordinator of research institutions, which includes the formulation, implementation, monitoring and evaluation of national research priorities.[38] The suggested solution is the creation of an endowment fund for research, as stated repeatedly by former Minister of Research and Technology, Bambang Brodjonegoro.[39]

In response to Law No. 11 of 2019 aimed at consolidating research under one national agency, some state ministries have changed the nomenclature on research units in their departments. Their research and development centres—Pusat Penelitian dan Pengembangan or Puslitbang—were dissolved and renamed. A majority use new names such as "Policy Assessment Centre" (Pusat Pengkajian Kebijakan) and their researchers are encouraged to change their status to that of policy analysts; the transfer of researchers into the new BRIN is voluntary.

Another notable mission of BRIN is to generate profit and attract investment.[40] We argue that this mission might shift the research agenda towards prioritizing research and innovation that potentially enhance the state economy. Also, BRIN is to internalize the Five Principles (Pancasila) as written in the Presidential Regulation Nos. 33 and 78 of 2021. Pancasila ideology as the foundation for national research has raised concerns among Indonesia's scientific community. There is a

---

[37] According to the KPK, the remainder is mostly spent on operational spending (30.68 per cent), services (13.17 per cent), capital spending (6.65 per cent), and training and education spending (5.77 per cent). See Gaudendius Suhardi, "Perpres BRIN Disandera", *Media Indonesia*, 11 February 2021, https://mediaindonesia.com/podiums/detail_podiums/2066-perpres-brin-disandera (accessed 30 July 2021).

[38] Gaudendius Suhardi, "Perpres BRIN Disandera".

[39] Bambang Brodjonegoro as quoted in Luky Maulana Firmansyah, "Lembaga Riset Independen Kunci Pengembangan Riset Nasional", *Lokadata.id*, 25 May 2020, https://lokadata.id/artikel/lembaga-riset-independen-kunci-pengembangan-riset-nasional (accessed 30 July 2021).

[40] Joko Widodo's ambition to build research powerhouse, CNBC Indonesia, "Mimpi Jokowi: Bangun Rumah Besar Penelitian".

question of whether this ideology will come to control all research in science and technology development.[41] The heavy influence of politics in the establishment of BRIN raises concerns that in the near future, the new agency will serve the economic and political interests of certain groups.

Another BRIN ambition—that of improving the management of the life sciences and intellectual property deriving from scientific research—is also seen as control over implementation. BRIN as a centralized research and innovation authority gives recommendations to the central government. It also acts as the national authority for research ethics approval, research data and publication repository through Repository Ilmiah Nasional or the National Scientific Repository, and as national research and technology innovation depository for patent or other types of intellectual property rights derived from scientific processes. The huge authority given to BRIN, combined with political support in the DPR RI, lacks mechanisms to check and balance its power.

Lastly, when BRIN is mandated to create and ensure a research and innovation ecosystem in the form of collaboration between government, researcher, and the business and industrial world, the position of basic research in the national research agenda in the future become a cause for concern.[42] Largely promoted as a triple-helix collaboration of research, this objective understates the important role and impact of science and technology on society and the environment. The objective prepares researchers to create output or innovation that are readily available for marketization in collaboration with business and industry. Behind

---

[41] Pramudya and Brata stated that "science and technology seems to be an autonomous world, in reality, within research institutions there are continuing political compromises and bargains"; in an online discussion "Membaca Arah Penggabungan Lembaga Penelitian Pemerintah", held by MINDSET Institute, 17 April 2021.

[42] CNBC Indonesia, Mimpi Jokowi: Bangun Rumah Besar Penelitian". The objective of science and technology institutions among others is to carry out research innovation to help business and industry strengthen increase the value add of Indonesia's resources.

this objective also lies an important issue of how commercialization of science, technology and innovation can only benefit businesses whose basic aim is to make profits, and not society in general, or the environment.[43]

POLITICS, TECHNOCRACY AND SCIENCE

The most debated issue after the release of Presidential Decree Nos. 33 and 78 of 2021 on BRIN was the role and influence of politics in the management of research and innovation.[44] This particularly refers to a point in the decree stating that the head of the supervisory board of BRIN will be the head of the Supervisory Board of BPIP, currently Megawati Soekarnoputri (chairperson of the PDI-P). She will therefore automatically become the head of the supervisory board of BRIN. As stated in the regulation, the supervisory board "has the authority to provide direction, input, evaluation, approval or policy recommendations and in certain circumstances can form a Special Task Force to streamline the implementation of tasks and functions carried out by the Executive" (Article 7).

The debate revolves around whether the PDI-P or the government will indoctrinate researchers and force them to follow and adopt the ideology and concept of nationalism of the PDI-P; whether research institutes and agencies would become political tools or, even worse, a venue to

---

[43] See Samuel Randalls, "Weather Profits: Weather Derivatives and the Commercialization of Meteorology", *Social Studies of Science* 40, no. 5 (October 2010): 705–30; Walter Block, "Katrina: Private Enterprise, the Dead Hand of the Past, and Weather Socialism: An Analysis in Economic Geography", *Ethics, Place and Environment* 9, no. 2 (2006): 231–41.

[44] The authors are aware that in addition to this political issue, there are other challenges for BRIN. One of them is the management or organization of BRIN itself. As stated in the Law on Sinas Iptek, BRIN is mandated to "integrate" state research agencies (LPNK) and ministries' R&Ds. This integration is not simple and will be arduous. There would be administrative consequences before the agency can be fully operational. Thanks to reviewers for underlining this issue.

channel government funds to political campaigns; whether Megawati is suitable as chair of the supervisory board of the national research agency; whether the government intends to emulate China in the management of research institutions, i.e., with its state ideology, or adopt a more liberal system like that in the United States.[45]

The newly appointed head of BRIN, L.T. Handoko, on various occasions, have tried to underline the positive impacts of the involvement of politics in BRIN by stating that this involvement can be seen as political support for science and research development in the country. Once, he stated that "In fact, the existence of the Supervisory Board, as in other countries, is to show the country's political commitment to support research ... in this country, it is only this time that research and innovation [is] strongly supported by government, not by individual, but by system."[46] He also underlines the role of Megawati and BPIP in making sure that national research would not deviate from Pancasila. "Research and knowledge can go anywhere. It can make nuclear bombs or human cloning. It is in the context of keeping research and knowledge from straying away from the Pancasila ideology that the existence of the Steering Committee is needed," says Handoko.[47]

In addition to guiding research in accordance with national ideology, Handoko further states that the involvement of Megawati can also be

---

[45] Some of the criticism and questions regarding the politicization of BRIN can be found in "Buyarnya Mimpi Teknokrat Pembentuk Ide BRIN. Saatnya Komunitas Ilmiah Berhenti Naif dan Anti-Politik", *The Conversation*, 29 April 2021, https://theconversation.com/buyarnya-mimpi-teknokrat-pembentuk-ide-brin-saatnya-komunitas-ilmiah-berhenti-naif-dan-anti-politik-159913. Also, "BRIN di Bawah Megawati Rentan Dipolitisasi & Rusak Iklim Ilmiah?", *Tirto.id*, 3 May 2021, https://tirto.id/gewN (accessed 30 July 2021).

[46] "Kepala BRIN: Kenapa Ribut? Ini Kan Cuma Dewan Pengarah", *Alinea.id*, 10 September 2021, https://www.alinea.id/nasional/kepala-brin-kenapa-ribut-ini-kan-cuma-dewan-pengarah-b2cAy960b (accessed 16 September 2021).

[47] "5 Fakta Megawati Jadi Kedua Dewan Pengawas BRIN", *Kumparan.com*, 1 May 2021, https://kumparan.com/kumparannews/5-fakta-megawati-jadi-ketua-dewan-pengawas-brin-1vehrVytHXd/full (accessed 30 July 2021).

seen positively as political support for research and innovation, so that researchers can focus on knowledge, innovation and invention, while political matters would become the responsibility of politicians.[48] In some discussions, Handoko preferred to discuss collaboration between state research agency and the private sector, the development of the research ecosystem towards global standards, and the contribution of research to the national economy.

The question of the relation between science and state has been looming over the country since Independence in 1945. This particularly relates to the persistent involvement of the government in the development and management of research under various regimes. After Independence, particularly during the Sukarno era, Indonesian scientists were required to make all their research "reflect the national tendencies of Indonesia" or that scientists are "responsible for articulating 'Indonesian Socialism' under Sukarno's Guided Democracy".[49] Under the New Order, science is no longer for science, but must be shifted to "Science for Development".[50] These conditions contributed to the "the failure of the enlightenment in Indonesia", echoing the title of Goss's book, leading to Indonesian research and innovation being left behind, even when compared to younger neighbouring countries such as Singapore and Malaysia.

The involvement of politics or the state in the management of research is sometimes referred to as "*haluan negara*" (national tendencies) or "*haluan ideologi Pancasila*" (state ideology). "Following national tendencies" is often interpreted even more narrowly as the interests of the dominant political party at the time.

---

[48] "BRIN Membutuhkan Dukungan Politik", *Tempo*, https://majalah.tempo.co/read/wawancara/163253/wawancara-kepala-brin-laksana-tri-handoko-dari-diaspora-peneliti-unggul-hingga-pentingnya-dukungan-politik; "Megawati Jadi Dewan Pengarah BRIN, Sekjen PDIP: Dia Penggagasnya", *Idntimes.com*, 3 May 2021, https://www.idntimes.com/news/indonesia/teatrika/megawati-jadi-dewan-pengarah-brin-sekjen-pdip-dia-penggagasnya/2 (accessed 30 July 2021).

[49] Goss, *The Floracrats*, pp. 136 and 158.

[50] Ibid., p. 167.

The involvement of politics certainly has an impact on the research ecosystem, i.e., the condition and environment that make research and innovation possible. It includes research funding, research collaboration, and the existence of an academic community. A good research ecosystem would provide academics and researchers the room to determine academic standards without political interference, including in the management of academic titles. In the past, the government could censor academic publication, prohibit certain kinds of research topics, and even fire those considered breaching national ideology.

The recent cases of the involvement of politics can be seen from the regulation relating to collaboration with foreign researchers and institutions. One of BRIN's responsibilities is to scrutinize and provide permits for foreign researchers to conduct research in Indonesia. Sometimes, the decision for the issuance of permits is not merely based on academic considerations, but political considerations with the involvement of the National Intelligence Agency (BIN).

In a country like Indonesia, the idea of the involvement of politics or political parties in the management of science and research does not always come from the politicians themselves. As elaborated earlier, during the process of proposing the law on research, it was researchers who invited politicians to be involved, partly to secure funding and partly to provide political support.

In sum, the relationship between science and politics is a complicated matter. It can be positive and negative at the same time. Heim et.al. confirms this through their statement: "The relationship between science and society should be seen not only in terms of politics influencing science, or even science influencing politics, but more with the two serving as mutual resources for each other."[51] This can be used as a platform for understanding the ambivalence of the involvement of ideology in science and innovation.

---

[51] Susanne Heim, Carola Sachse and Mark Walker, *The Kaiser Wilhelm Society under National Socialism* (Cambridge: Cambridge University Press, 2009), p. 1.

CONCLUSION

The establishment of BRIN in 2021 marks the transformation of Indonesia's science and technology management. Despite the long history of many of the institutions that merged under BRIN, such as LIPI, BPPT, LAPAN, BATAN, Eijkman, and the Kemenristek-Dikti, these institutions are being remade. The ambition of BRIN to become the only scientific authority in Indonesia still faces the huge challenge of consolidating different institutions that have different organizational characteristics. Currently, the main challenge faced by BRIN is institutional transition. The merger of four main research institutions and research and development units from different state ministries is BRIN's main agenda in the near future. During the transition years, BRIN must handle the bureaucratic and technocratic problems involved, such as the transfer of government researchers into BRIN and BRIN's organizational arrangement.

The second challenge is the politicization of science, something which in the past had slowed Indonesian research and innovation. BRIN's process of creation itself showed that science and politics cannot be separated. At its birth, BRIN needed politics to secure its position among state organizations, even as political and market ideologies also crept into the vision of the newly established research institutions. This seems inevitable, and Indonesia's experience has proven this quite vividly. The political regime always positions science as one of its instruments of power. We saw this phenomenon for example in the political slogans of earlier regimes. In the period of Sukarno, "science must embody Indonesian socialism", while Suharto's New Order proclaimed "science for development".

Thus, research cannot be separated from politics. The policy of scientific development needs political support, be it from the President or the People's Representatives Body (DPR). However, scientific development must be put in a long-term perspective, in a bigger framework beyond political premises.

Lastly, the scientific ecosystem relies closely on several factors. First, the national leadership has to hold a long-term vision to develop science and technology and advance basic research for the application of technology and innovation. Second, research institutions must debureaucratize in order to enable researchers to produce publications and technological innovations for the greater good. Third, and lastly, funds and budgetary support are needed for both basic and advanced or applied sciences, including the social sciences and the humanities.